thgow
palooza readers

A Den, a Tree, a Nest Is Best

By Katharine Kenah

School Specialty.
Publishing

Text Copyright © 2006 School Specialty Publishing. Marsupial Sue Character © 2001 by John Lithgow. Marsupial Sue
Illustration © 2001 by Jack E. Davis.

Library of Congress Cataloging-in-Publication Data is on file with the publisher.

Send all inquiries to:
School Specialty Publishing
8720 Orion Place
Columbus, OH 43240-2111

ISBN 0-7696-4263-2

1 2 3 4 5 6 7 8 9 10 PHXBK 10 09 08 07 06 05

Table of Contents

Den

Where does a fox live?
In a **den**!

A den is a living space
made by animals.
Most dens are dug out of the ground.
Some dens are in **caves**,
hollow trees, and rocky places.
Foxes often move into dens
that have been left by other animals.
They dig extra tunnels and rooms
for sleeping and storing food.

Marsupial Sue Shares

A den may be up to 75 feet long! This is almost as long as
a basketball court.

Shell

Where does a giant tortoise live?
In a shell!

A shell is a home that moves with its owner.
It covers an animal's soft body
and keeps it safe.
A turtle's shell is part of its skeleton.
It is made of two parts.
The outside is made of hard skin.
The inside is made of bone.
When danger is near, a turtle pulls
its head, legs, and tail inside its shell
to stay safe.

Marsupial Sue Shares

The shells of sea turtles are flatter than the shells of land turtles.
A sea turtle cannot pull itself inside its shell.

Tree

Where does a koala live?
In a tree!

Eucalyptus trees are homes for koalas.
They grow in Australia.
Koalas sleep most of each day
in the branches of these trees.
They get food and water
from eating the long green leaves.
Koalas climb down from one tree
only to move into another!

Marsupial Sue Shares

Koala comes from an Australian aborigine word that means
"no drink." Koalas rarely drink water. They get the water they
need from eating tree leaves.

Nest

Where does a bird live?
In a nest!

Nests are made of grass, mud, leaves,
and twigs.
Birds build nests in the country
and in the city.
They build nests in trees, bushes, cliffs, caves,
barns, birdhouses, and on windowsills.
A nest is a safe place to lay eggs.
Most nests are shaped like bowls,
so eggs cannot roll out and break.
Baby birds are weak and helpless.
A nest gives them a place to grow strong.

Marsupial Sue Shares

Some hummingbird nests are only one inch tall—shorter than
a blade of grass!

Burrow

Where does a prairie dog live?
In a **burrow**!

A burrow is a hole or tunnel
in the ground made by an animal.
Prairie dogs dig lots of burrows
close together.
These groups of burrows
are **towns** or colonies.
Each burrow has two openings.
Prairie dogs come out of their burrows
to look for food and to watch for enemies.

Marsupial Sue Shares

There may be up to 500 prairie dogs living in one colony.

Cave

Where does a bat live?
In a cave!

A cave is an opening
in the side of a hill or mountain.
Some caves are small.
Some caves go on for miles and miles.
A really large, underground cave
is a cavern.
Caves are quiet, warm, and dark.
During the day, bats sleep hanging
upside-down in a cave.
At night, they fly out to search for bugs.

Marsupial Sue Shares

The Carlsbad Caverns in New Mexico were discovered after
thousands of bats flew out of the cave at dusk. From a distance,
they looked like smoke rising in the air.

Hive

Where does a honeybee live?
In a **hive**!

For a honeybee, a hive is a home
and a place to store things.
A hive is full of honeycombs.
Honeycombs are like walls of wax
with tiny round spaces in them.
The spaces are **cells**.
When a hive is full of busy honeybees,
the cells are full of honey, eggs,
and baby bees.

Marsupial Sue Shares

All the bees in one hive have the same smell. Guard bees will attack outside bees that do not have this smell!

Colony

Where does a puffin live?
In a colony!

A colony is a large group
of the same kind of animal
living together.
Puffins live in colonies on islands
and rocky coasts where the sea is cold.
They lay their eggs in holes under rocks
and at the end of tunnels in the dirt.
Each pair of puffins has its own burrow,
but the whole colony works together
to guard its eggs and its young.

Marsupial Sue Shares

Puffins swim under the water, similar to how birds fly in the air.
They stroke with their wings and steer with their feet.

Coral Reef

Where does a sea anemone live?
On a **coral reef**!

A coral reef is like an underwater fish city.
It is made from the skeletons
of millions of tiny sea animals.
And it is a home for millions
of living ones, too!
A sea anemone looks like a flower,
but it is really an animal.
One end of the sea anemone
attaches to a coral reef.
The other end catches food that drifts by.

Marsupial Sue Shares

The longest coral reef in the world is the Great Barrier Reef
of Australia. It is 1,250 miles long—the distance from Chicago to Miami!

Web

Where does a spider live?
On a **web**!

A web is made of silky strings.
Spiders have **spinnerets**
on their bodies.
Spiders produce silk threads from these parts.
The silk flows out at first.
Then, it becomes firm.
Spiders use webs to catch food.
Bugs get stuck in the sticky web
and cannot escape.
Spiders make webs in all different
shapes and sizes.

Marsupial Sue Shares
Spider silk is the strongest thread or fiber in nature.

Coop

Where does a chicken live?
In a **coop**!

A coop is a cage used to house small animals.
It is often made from wooden boards
and wire.
Coops give animals a place to eat and sleep.
Coops protect animals from **predators**.
Coops keep animals from running away.
Chickens in small coops
lay their eggs in straw.
Coops keep chickens warm and dry.

Marsupial Sue Shares

A hen can lay up to 245 eggs a year!

Stall

Where does a horse live?
In a **stall**!

A stall is a room for a horse.
Most stalls are in barns.
A good stall is clean
with lots of fresh air and sunlight.
A low door on a gate opens
to let the horse come and go.
Straw keeps the floor soft and dry.
Horses eat and sleep in their stalls.

Marsupial Sue Shares

Horses often sleep standing up. A horse can even sleep
with its eyes open!

Aquarium

Where does a fish live?
In an **aquarium**!

An aquarium is a tank or bowl
filled with water that is used
to house animals and plants.
An animal or plant that lives
in water is **aquatic**.
Most aquariums are made of glass.
Sand and small stones cover the bottom.
A light keeps the water warm.
A filter keeps the water clean.
An aquarium makes a good home for a fish.

Marsupial Sue Shares

Fish and plants keep each other healthy. Fish breathe the oxygen given off by the plants. Plants take in the carbon dioxide given off by the fish.

Vocabulary

aquarium–a tank or bowl filled with water that holds fish and plants. *We put new fish in the classroom aquarium.*

aquatic–an animal or plant that lives in water. *A fish is an aquatic animal.*

burrow–a hole or tunnel in the ground made by an animal as a living space. *I saw a prairie dog by its burrow.*

cave–a hollow or opening in the side of a hill or mountain. *The bats flew out of the cave at dusk.*

cell–the tiny, round hole in a honeycomb. *Each honeycomb cell was full of honey.*

coop–an enclosure used to confine small animals. *Dad's in the chicken coop collecting eggs.*

coral reef–an underwater ridge or mound made up of the skeletons of millions of coral. *The coral reef is full of fish*

den–a living space made and used by animals as a shelter. *The bear cubs spent the winter sleeping in their den.*

eucalyptus–a tree that is native to Australia and provides shelter and food for koalas. *Koalas sleep in the eucalyptus tree.*

hive–a shelter that houses a colony of bees. *Hannah's class saw honeybees flying out of the hive.*

predator–an animal that hunts and eats other animals. *A chicken in its coop is safe from predators.*

spinneret–the structure on a spider's body that produces silk thread. *Silk threads shot from the spider's spinnerets.*

stall–a room for a domestic animal in a barn or shed. *The horse needs fresh straw for its stall.*

town–a group of prairie dog burrows, also called a colony. *The prairie dog town had over 20 burrows.*

web–a structure made of silk threads spun by a spider. *The morning dew sparkled on the spider's web.*

Think About It!

1. Which animal lives in a shell? Can you think of other animals that live in shells?

2. Do prairie dogs live alone or with other prairie dogs?

3. Do koalas drink lots of water? Why or why not?

4. Do bats ever leave their caves? When?

5. What do honeybees store in the cells of their honeycombs?

The Story and You!

1. How would your life be different if you lived in a tree? How would it be different if you lived in a cave?

2. Think of three good things about an animal having a shell.

3. How are fishing poles similar to spider webs?

4. If you were a bird, how would you design your nest? How would it be shaped? What would it be made of?

5. How is an apartment building like a colony?